Sewing from Square One

Sewing from Square One

TURN SIMPLE FABRIC SQUARES INTO 20 PROJECTS

DARLENE CAHILL

Creative Publishing international
Chanhassen, MN

Acknowledgments

My heartfelt thanks to the wonderful friends and colleagues who have helped create
this book, including the CPi staff, photographer Tim Boyles, my sewing assistant
Sandy Young, and Lorraine Montgomery for organizing and support of many kinds.
Thank you, Euro-pro sewing machines and the Home Shopping Network,
for the many opportunities you have given me. A special thank you to my wonderful
husband George Cahill for gifting me with the name of the book and heaping lavish
words of encouragement on me to follow through and complete this project.

**Creative Publishing
international**

Copyright 2006
Creative Publishing international, Inc.
18705 Lake Drive East
Chanhassen, Minnesota 55317
1-800-328-3895
www.creativepub.com
All rights reserved

President/CEO: Ken Fund
Executive Editor: Alison Brown Cerier
Senior Editor: Linda Neubauer
Photo Stylist: Joanne Wawra
Creative Director: Brad Springer
Photo Art Director: Tim Himsel
Photographer: Steve Galvin
Author portrait photographer: Tim Boyles
Production Manager: Linda Halls
Cover Design: Lois Stanfield
Interior Design: Terry Patton Rhoads

Printed in USA
10 9 8 7 6 5 4 3 2 1

Library of Congress Cataloging-in-
Publication Data

Cahill, Darlene
  Sewing from square one : 20 pattern-free
projects you can do / Darlene Cahill.
      p. cm.
   ISBN-13: 978-1-58923-275-4 (soft cover)
   ISBN-10: 1-58923-275-5 (soft cover)
   1. Sewing. 2. Household linens. 3. Dress
   accessories. I. Title.
   TT705.C32 2006
   646.2--dc22
2005037242

Contents

Darlene Cahill has been the sewing expert at Home Shopping Network for more than nine years, demonstrating a multitude of products while sharing projects and tips with viewers. Her passion for sewing comes from years as a costume designer, dressmaker, and interior decorator. Darlene was also a singer/dancer/actress and she performed across a broad spectrum of the entertainment industry, from her own touring magical variety act to the CBS reality show *Wickedly Perfect*.

Sewing Is Fun!

My passion is showing people how much fun they can have sewing, even if they've never sewn before. For some years now, I've been on the Home Shopping Network, hosting programs about sewing machines and products. I show how to make creative projects and share lots of tips to make sewing easy and successful.

I've written *Sewing from Square One* so you can join the fun, too. Here are twenty of my favorite quick-and-easy projects. Each starts with a square (or rectangle) of fabric— it's magical how that square turns into anything from a napkin to a skirt! There are no curved seams to match, no complicated fitting, no patterns to buy. There are projects for home décor, apparel, and craft items you can sew for yourself or as gifts for your family and friends.

The title *Sewing from Square One* also has a second meaning: you can start from square one, the very beginning, and make anything in this book. All you need are a conventional sewing machine and a few sewing supplies. (If you have a serger, feel free to use it for rolled hems or seam finishes, but it's not necessary for these projects.) There are step-by-step directions with how-to photos. Each project includes a list of materials to buy or gather. And I share lots of my favorite sewing tips and tricks.

A basics section beginning on page 88 covers fabrics, tools, and skills like sewing seams. I recommend reading through it before you start a project. While you are working on a project, if you come to a sewing term you don't quite understand, just check the explanations at the back of the book.

The most important thing is to have fun, from choosing the fabrics to adding your finishing touches. Get creative and personalize your projects with embellishments and decorative stitching. You'll be amazed at what you can do.

Reversible Placemats

Two placemats in one! Just flip over the placemat for a different look. You can even make one side with a holiday fabric and the other side for everyday suppers. The following instructions are for basic rectangular placemats. To give them a little padding and body, I've used prequilted fabric on one side. Placemats can be any shape, size, or style, depending on your table and personal taste. Cut off the four corners to make octagons, or round off the corners to ovals. If you like it, it's perfect!

YOU'LL NEED

For two placemats:

- ☐ ½ yd. (0.5 m) fabric for placemat front
- ☐ ½ yd. (0.5 m) prequilted cotton for placemat back
- ☐ Tape measure or yardstick (meterstick)
- ☐ Pencil or other fabric marker
- ☐ Scissors

- ☐ Rotary cutter, cutting mat, and straightedge, optional
- ☐ Iron and ironing board
- ☐ Pins
- ☐ Thread
- ☐ Sewing machine
- ☐ Hand needle

LET'S GET SEWING

1 Cut two rectangles of the front fabric and two of the back fabric, each 19" wide × 13" long (48.5 × 33 cm).

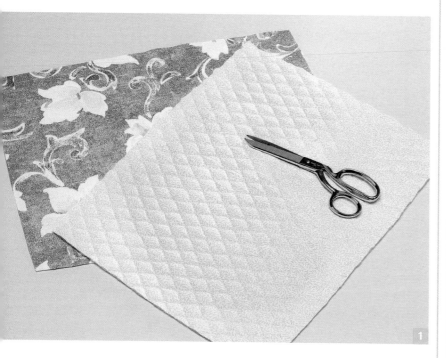

2 Place a front and back right side together and pin around the edge every few inches.

3 Sew a ½" (1.3 cm) seam around the edge, starting just past the center of one long side.

4 Stop stitching with the needle down in the fabric ½" (1.3 cm) from the corner. Raise the presser foot, turn the fabric, lower the presser foot, and continue sewing. Pivoting like this will give your placemat sharp, square corners.

5 Finish sewing the seam, pivoting at each corner as in step 4. Stop stitching 3" (7.5 cm) from where you started to leave an opening for turning the placemat right side out.

6 Trim the corners diagonally within ⅛" (3 mm) of the stitching at each corner, using scissors. This reduces the fabric bulk to make the corners nice and square.

7 Turn the placemat right side out and press the outer edge. Press the seam allowances toward the inside at the opening. Slipstitch the opening closed.

8 Thread the machine with the top thread matching the placemat front and the bobbin thread matching the placemat back. Topstitch ½" (1.3 cm) from the edge all around the placemat.

Enjoy your placemats and have a wonderful celebration!

Darlene's Tips

■ You can use one of your machine's decorative stitches to topstitch the placemats.

■ Before turning the placemat right side out, press one upper seam allowance back. This will give you a neater edge on the outside.

Napkins and Table Topper

Cloth napkins make every meal seem special, and you can save trees, too! You can whip up a set of napkins with very little time or money. I think store-bought napkins are too small, so I super-size mine. A table topper is made the same way as a napkin, only larger. You can use a topper alone over a round table for a bistro effect, or put one over a plain tablecloth to add color and personality to a table. If your dining table is long, put two or three toppers down the center.

YOU'LL NEED

- ☐ 1⅓ yd. (1.23 m) fabric for four napkins
- ☐ 1 yd. (0.92 m) fabric for table topper
- ☐ Tape measure or yardstick (meterstick)
- ☐ Pencil or other fabric marker
- ☐ Scissors
- ☐ Rotary cutter, cutting mat, and straightedge, optional
- ☐ Iron and ironing board
- ☐ Pins
- ☐ Thread
- ☐ Sewing machine

1 Cut four 21" (53.5 cm) squares for napkins. For a table topper, cut a square 1" (2.5 cm) larger than your desired finished size.

2 With the wrong side of the napkin or topper facing up, beginning along one side, fold the edge over ¼" (6 mm) and crease the fold with your fin-gers. Then fold the edge over ¼" (6 mm) again, and crease, forming a double-fold hem.

3 Sew along the inner fold of the hem all the way down the side, folding and finger-pressing as you go. Stop sewing 2" (5 cm) from the first corner with the needle down in the fabric.

4 Fold in the hem to the corner. Then fold the corner diagonally ½" (1.3 cm) from the end creating a small triangle at the corner.

5 Finger-press the double-fold hem into the next side, including the folded triangle at the corner. Continue sewing along the first side until the needle penetrates the center fold of the mitered corner. Stop with the needle down in the fabric, and raise the presser foot.

6 Turn the napkin or topper a quarter turn. Lower the presser foot and continue sewing, finger-pressing the double-fold hem as you go and forming miters at each corner.

7 When you reach the place where you started, just overlap a few stitches, and you're done.

Now wasn't that easy? Your table linens look very professional!

Darlene's Tips

■ Always hold the thread tails as you start to sew. This prevents threads from becoming tangled at the beginning of the stitching line and gives you a cleaner, more professional look.

■ Natural fibers like linen, cotton, and cotton-blended fabrics absorb liquids better than synthetic fabrics do, so they make better napkins. It is also much easier to finger-press the double-fold hems in natural-fiber fabrics. The only drawback is that cotton and linen napkins require pressing after laundering for a nice crisp look.

Duvet Cover

A duvet cover is like a large pillowcase that covers a comforter. It can be difficult to buy just the right duvet cover for your bedroom, but now you can make your own. With a buttoned opening on the back, the duvet cover completely encloses the comforter, yet comes off easily for washing.

The sewing steps are not difficult, but you'll be working with a lot of fabric, so find a space to spread out. Fabrics are usually not wide enough to make a duvet cover with one width, so you will sew long pieces together. For a professional look, use one full width of fabric down the center of the duvet cover front and sew equal narrow strips to the sides. If you purchase a decorator print, buy one additional pattern repeat to make sure you will be able to match the design at the seams. The back, cut from two equal pieces of plain cotton fabric, can be sewn down the center.

YOU'LL NEED

Twin size:
- ☐ 5 yd. (4.6 m) fabric for front
- ☐ 5¼ yd. (4.8 m) fabric for back

Standard/queen size:
- ☐ 5 ½ yd. (5.05 m) fabric for front
- ☐ 5¾ yd. (5.3 m) fabric for back

King size:
- ☐ 5 ½ yd. (5.05 m) fabric, at least 54" (137 cm) wide, for front
- ☐ 5¾ yd. (5.3 m) fabric, at least 54" (137 cm) wide, for back

For all sizes:
- ☐ Tape measure or yardstick (meterstick)
- ☐ Pencil or other fabric marker
- ☐ Scissors
- ☐ Rotary cutter, cutting mat, and straightedge, optional
- ☐ Iron and ironing board
- ☐ Pins
- ☐ Thread
- ☐ Sewing machine and button attachment presser foot
- ☐ Seam ripper
- ☐ Buttons

Darlene's Tips

■ If you want to make a duvet cover for a twin or standard size bed and you don't have to match a print, plan the pieces so the seams fall at the edge of the bed rather than off the sides. Be sure to allow for seam allowances when cutting the pieces.

1 Measure the length of your comforter and add 1" (2.5 cm) to determine how long to cut the pieces for the front. Mark the cut length of the first piece along the selvage. Then mark the cut locations for the second piece, beginning and ending at the same locations in the pattern repeat as the first piece. Carefully mark the lines across the entire fabric, making sure they are perpendicular to the selvages. When you are sure of your measurements and sure that the pattern will line up across the seams, cut the pieces.

2 Cut one of the front pieces in half on the lengthwise grain (parallel to the selvages).

3 Place a narrow piece over a full-width piece, right sides together, aligning the selvages. Fold back the upper selvage until the pattern matches. Adjust the top layer up or down so the pattern lines up exactly. Press the fold line. Then unfold and pin the layers together down the fold line.

4 Stitch the layers together, following the fold line. Remove the pins as you come to them.

5 Check that the pattern matches on the right side. Trim away the selvages, leaving ½" (1.3 cm) seam allowances.

6 Repeat steps 3 to 5 to join the other narrow strip to the opposite side of the full-width strip. Trim the sides of the duvet cover equally so the duvet cover front is 1" (2.5 cm) wider than the width of your comforter.

7 Cut the duvet cover back fabric in half on the crosswise grain (perpendicular to the selvages) to make two full-width pieces. Sew them together along one long edge. Trim the sides equally so the duvet cover back is 1" (2.5 cm) wider than your comforter.

8 Cut across the duvet cover back 16" (40.5 cm) from the top. Press under ½" (1.3 cm) on both cut edges. Then press under 2" (5 cm) and pin. Stitch along the inner folds of each piece to make hems.

9 Mark buttonhole positions every 5" to 6" (12.7 to 15 cm) in the hem of the short piece. Sew buttonholes, following the instructions in your sewing machine manual.

10 Insert a pin across the end of a buttonhole. Using your seam ripper, cut the buttonhole open. The pin will prevent you from accidentally cutting too far.

11 Lap the hem of the short piece over the hem of the long piece. Baste the layers together at the sides. Mark through the buttonholes for button placement on the lower hem.

12 Set the sewing machine to zigzag in place. Using the button attachment presser foot, sew buttons at the marks.

13 Button the duvet cover back pieces together. Center the front, facedown, over the back, aligning the upper edges. Trim away excess fabric on the bottom of the back. Pin the layers together on all four sides.

14 Sew a ½" (1.3 cm) seam around the outer edges, pivoting with the needle down in the fabric at the corners. Trim the seam allowances at the corners diagonally within ⅛" (3 mm) of the stitching.

15 Unbutton the duvet cover and turn it right side out. Press the outer edges. Insert your comforter and button the cover closed. Spread it on your bed and see how it changes the whole room!

Can you believe you did that? I can!

Darlene's Tips

■ Large patterns are easier to match but they require more fabric. Buy at least one extra repeat of the fabric to be sure you have enough to match the seams.

■ If you purchased washable fabric and plan to wash the cover, you should launder and press the fabric before cutting the pieces. If you plan to dry-clean the cover, you can start right away.

■ You can add a decorator touch by stitching fabric-covered welting (also called piping) into the long seams and around the edges of your duvet cover. This will add interest, dimension, and contrast and may help to forgive a seam that isn't matched to absolute perfection! (See pages 22 and 23 for how-to steps.)

Pillow Shams

Today's bedding doesn't seem complete without the addition of a coordinating sham. Shams dress the bed while they protect and hide the bed pillow. You can insert piping, fringe, or lace around the edge, depending on your décor. This design has a flange, an extension around the outer edge, which helps to make an upscale statement as it extends the size of the pillow.

YOU'LL NEED

- ☐ 1 yd. (0.92 m) decorator fabric for the front
- ☐ 1 yd. (0.92 m) coordinating fabric for the back
- ☐ 3½ yd. (3.2 m) fabric-covered welting (piping)
- ☐ Tape measure or yardstick (meterstick)
- ☐ Pencil or other fabric marker
- ☐ Scissors
- ☐ Rotary cutter, cutting mat, and straightedge, optional
- ☐ Iron and ironing board
- ☐ Pins
- ☐ Thread
- ☐ Sewing machine and welting or zipper foot
- ☐ Standard size bed pillow

1 For a standard pillow size, cut a 33" × 26" (84 × 66 cm) rectangle of decorator fabric for the sham front. Cut two 20" × 26" (51 × 66 cm) rectangles of coordinating fabric for the sham back.

2 Place the two back pieces over the front piece, aligning the outer edges. Mark the two edges that overlap down the center of the back.

3 Fold under ½" (1.3 cm) twice on each marked edge and stitch along the inner fold to make a double-fold hem. Set the pieces aside.

4 Attach a welting or zipper foot to the machine. Machine-baste the welting to the edge of the sham front, matching the raw edges. Clip up to, but not through, the stitching on the welting at the corners, so the seam allowances will spread open to turn the corner. Where the ends overlap, turn back the fabric that covers the cording. Cut the cording so the ends just meet. Then wrap the fabric back over the cording, overlapping the ends, and finish stitching.

5 Pin the sham back pieces over the front, right sides together, matching the outer edges and overlapping the hemmed edges down the middle.

6 Sew a ½" (1.3 cm) seam around the edge, still using the welting or zipper foot, and catching the welting between the front and back.

7 Turn the sham right side out, and press.

8 Mark a line 2" (5 cm) from the welted edge all around the sham front. Pin along the line through both layers. Straight stitch over the marked line, pulling out the pins as you come to them. You just made a flanged edge!

9 Tuck the pillow into the sham through the opening in the back. Plump it up and prop it at the head of the bed.

Doesn't your new sham look great? And think of the money you've saved!

Darlene's Tips

■ If your pillow is quite plump, the back opening may gap apart. Stitch Velcro on the overlapping edges of the opening to keep them closed.

■ For a professional look, always center a printed design on your pillow sham.

Decorator Pillow

Pillows are an easy, quick project for beginners. By simply sewing four straight lines and stuffing to your heart's content, anyone of any age or skill level can enjoy the artistic satisfaction and money savings that come with making pillows. There is no right or wrong in the world of pillows. For me, the more embellishment, the better! This style features triangles made from, of course, squares.

YOU'LL NEED

- ☐ ½ yd. (0.5 m) decorator fabric in a lighter color or solid
- ☐ ½ yd. (0.5 m) decorator fabric in a darker color or print
- ☐ 2 ⅛ yd. (1.95 m) decorative cord welting, optional
- ☐ 18" (46 cm) pillow form or bag of polyester fiberfill
- ☐ Tape measure or yardstick (meterstick)

- ☐ Pencil or other fabric marker
- ☐ Scissors
- ☐ Rotary cutter, cutting mat, and straightedge, optional
- ☐ Iron and ironing board
- ☐ Pins
- ☐ Thread
- ☐ Sewing machine and welting or zipper foot
- ☐ Hand needle

1 Cut a 13" (33 cm) square of each decorator fabric for the pieced front of the pillow. The pillow back will be cut in step 6.

2 Fold each square in half diagonally, and cut along the fold line. You now have four triangles, two of each fabric.

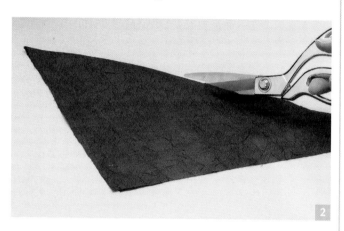

3 Pin two contrasting triangles, right sides together, along one 13" (33 cm) side, and stitch a ½" (1.3 cm) seam. Reverse the order of the fabrics and repeat with the remaining two triangles. You should now have two two-toned triangles that are opposites. Press the seam allowances open.

4 Pin the two pieced triangles, right sides together, on the long edge, being careful to match up the center seam exactly. Stitch a ½" (1.3 cm) seam to complete the pillow front. Press the seam allowances open.

5 Mark the fabric edge ½" (1.3 cm) from each corner. From each mark, draw a line that tapers to the fabric edge 4" (10 cm) from the corner. Trim each corner on the lines. This will make the finished pillow appear more square and eliminate what I call "cat ear corners."

6 Using this pillow front as a pattern, cut one piece of fabric for the pillow back. To make a pillow without welting, omit step 7.

7 Attach a welting or zipper foot to the sewing machine. Machine-baste the welting to the edge of the pillow front. Where the ends overlap, recoil the cord plies to make the welting look continuous.

8 Pin the pillow back over the front, right sides together, aligning the edges.

9 Sew a ½" (1.3 cm) seam around the edge, catching the welting between the layers. Pivot with the needle down in the fabric at each corner, and leave an 8" (20.5 cm) opening for turning.

10 Trim the corners diagonally to within ⅛" (3 mm) of the stitching. Turn the pillow cover right side out.

11 Insert a purchased pillow form or stuff the pillow with loose polyester fiberfill.

12 Pin the opening closed. Slipstitch the opening closed by hand.

Now kick back and enjoy your new creation!

Darlene's Tips

■ When matching two seam lines that cross each other, pin the layers together directly into the center of the seam. Slow down the machine as you get close to the seams and make sure the seam allowances on the underside are still pressed open. Remove the pin just before you get to it.

■ Stuff balls of fiberfill tightly into the corners of your pillow so they don't get limp later.

■ Trim the edge of your pillow with brush fringe instead of welting, following the same steps. To keep the fringe under control, don't remove the chainstitch on the fringe until you turn the pillow right side out. Then simply pull on the thread to release the chainstitch and fluff out the fringe.

Table Runners

Add elegance or a holiday look to your dining table with a runner. You can either line the runner with a coordinating fabric or simply hem the sides. Both styles have pointed ends with tassels that can drape over the table edge or just extend to the sides in the center of your table. The unlined style is a good choice for firm fabrics like tapestries or brocades. Lining will give extra body to lightweight or slippery fabrics.

Following the directions below, your table runner will be 13" (33 cm) wide and any length you wish. If you pick fabric that is 45" to 54" (115 to 137 cm) wide, you can cut three runners the length of your fabric. If your fabric is 60" (152.5 cm) wide, you can make four runners. Make matching runners for your dining table, a sofa table, and a buffet. Or make one for yourself and give the others as gifts.

Grab a tape measure and measure the width, length, or diameter of your table, depending on which way you'd like your runner to, well . . . RUN!

YOU'LL NEED

☐ Decorator fabric, amount depends on length of runner

☐ Coordinating lightweight fabric (same amount) for a lined runner

☐ Two tassels

☐ Tape measure or yardstick (meterstick)

☐ Pencil or other fabric marker

☐ Scissors

☐ Rotary cutter, cutting mat, and straightedge, optional

☐ Iron and ironing board

☐ Pins

☐ Thread

☐ Sewing machine

☐ Hand needle, for lined runner

Lined Table Runner

1 Measure how long you want your table runner to be, including any amount you want to extend over the table edge, usually 8" (20.5 cm) at each end. Cut a rectangle 1" (2.5 cm) longer than the desired finished length and 14" (35.5 cm) wide.

2 Mark the sides 7" (18 cm) from the ends; mark the center of the short ends. Draw lines from the side marks to the center, and cut the ends into points.

3 Use the runner front as a pattern to cut the runner lining.

4 Pin the runner front and lining right sides together. Pin a tassel at each point between the layers, with the top of the tassel ½" (1.3 cm) from the cut edges and the cord extending out.

5 Stitch a ½" (1.3 cm) seam around the runner through both layers, pivoting with the needle down in the fabric at the points and corners. Leave a 6" (15 cm) opening along one side for turning the runner right side out. Stitch again over the points to make sure the tassels are attached securely.

6 Turn the runner right side out. Press. Slipstitch the opening closed.

Unlined Table Runner

1 Determine how long you want your table runner to be, including any amount you want to extend over the table edge, usually 8" (20.5 cm) at each end. Cut a rectangle 1" (2.5 cm) longer than the desired finished length and 15" (38 cm) wide.

2 Turn under the long edges ½" (1.3 cm) and press. Turn under ½" (1.3 cm) again and press again to form double-fold hems. Stitch along the inner fold on each hem.

3 Fold one narrow end in half, right sides together. Pin a tassel between the layers, snug against the fold with the top of the tassel ½" (1.3 cm) from the cut edges and the cord extending out.

4 Stitch a ½" (1.3 cm) seam across the end. Backstitch at both ends, especially over the tassel cord.

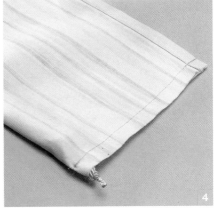

5 Trim off the folded corner diagonally to within ⅛" (3 mm) of the seam. Press the seam allowances open.

6 Repeat steps 3 to 5 on the opposite end of the runner. Turn the ends right side out and center the points. Press.

That's all there is to it!

Darlene's Tips

■ For a tailored look, instead of adding tassels, insert piping around the outer edge. Follow the directions on pages 22 and 23.

■ Instead of tassels, stitch decorator fringe along the angled ends of the table runner.

■ If you are serging a rolled hem into the edges of your table runner, put woolly nylon thread in the upper looper with its tension set on zero. Shorten your stitch length. The hem will look fuller than a conventional satin stitch.

Remote Control Holster

Ever find yourself shouting, "Where's the remote?" Then this project is for you. This holster goes over the arm of a sofa or chair and down under the seat cushion so it stays put. You can make five narrow pockets for holding all your remotes or make some pockets different sizes for holding pens, a phone, or the television guide. Match the fabric color to the couch so it blends nicely with the décor of the room or use a contrasting fabric for a "here I am" statement. When it's time to watch your favorite show, you'll know exactly where the remote is.

YOU'LL NEED

- ☐ 1 ¼ yd. (1.15 m) decorator fabric
- ☐ 1 ¼ yd. (1.15 m) coordinating fabric for lining
- ☐ Tape measure or yardstick (meterstick)
- ☐ Pencil or other fabric marker
- ☐ Scissors
- ☐ Rotary cutter, cutting mat, and straightedge, optional
- ☐ Iron and ironing board
- ☐ Pins
- ☐ Thread
- ☐ Sewing machine
- ☐ Hand needle

1 Cut two rectangles of fabric 38" × 22" (96.5 × 56 cm), one for the backing and one for the lining. Cut two rectangles 7" × 22" (18 × 56 cm) for the pocket and pocket lining.

2 Pin the pocket and pocket lining right sides together. Stitch a ½" (1.3 cm) seam along one long edge. Press the seam allowances open.

3 Fold the pocket wrong sides together. Roll the layers between your thumb and forefinger to ease the stitching line to the very top, and press the upper edge.

4 Add decorative topstitching to the upper edge, sewing down and encasing the seam allowances.

5 Pin the pocket to the lower edge of the backing piece, matching the bottom and sides. Machine-baste the pocket in place within the ½" (1.3 cm) seam allowance.

6 Place the backing and backing lining right sides together, and pin around the edges, enclosing the pocket between the layers.

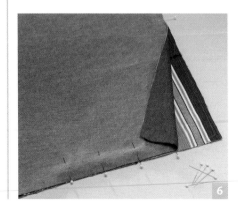

7 Stitch a ½" (1.3 cm) seam around the edges, pivoting with the needle down in the fabric at the corners and leaving a 6" (15 cm) opening along the top center.

8 Trim the corners diagonally to within ⅛" (3 mm) of the stitching. Turn the remote holster right side out.

9 Press the remote holster. Slip-stitch the opening closed.

10 Mark and pin every 4" (10 cm) across the top of the pocket, or wherever you want the pocket division lines to be.

11 Stitch vertical lines through all the layers at the marks, using a decorative stitch or triple straight stretch stitch to divide the pocket into sections.

12 Drape the remote holster over the arm of the sofa or chair and tuck the extension under the seat cushion.

Fill the pockets and settle in!

Darlene's Tips

■ You can reinforce the top of each stitching line on the pocket dividers with backstitching.

■ If 21" (53.5 cm) is too wide for the arm of your sofa, customize the size to fit. Make fewer pockets, if necessary.

■ Stitch up a matching pillow to help tie your remote holster into your décor.

■ If the holster slips from the weight of the remotes, use a strip of sticky Velcro along the end under the cushion.

Posh Poncho

Wear this flowing poncho over a camisole or a tank top. It is cut to drape on the bias, giving it a comfortable flow and a lyrical movement. For the most attractive drape, choose silk, chiffon, or crepe. Bead trim is the perfect finishing touch. If your fabric is 45" (115 cm) wide, your poncho will be shorter on one side, like this one. For a square poncho, buy fabric that is 54" to 60" (137 to 152.5 cm) wide.

YOU'LL NEED

- ☐ ⅞ yd. (0.8 m) sheer or semisheer fabric for outer poncho
- ☐ ⅞ yd. (0.8 m) matching solid fabric for lining
- ☐ 4 yd. (3.7 m) beaded trim
- ☐ Tape measure or yardstick (meterstick)
- ☐ Pencil or other fabric marker
- ☐ Scissors
- ☐ Rotary cutter, cutting mat, and straightedge, optional
- ☐ Iron and ironing board
- ☐ Dinner plate
- ☐ Pins
- ☐ Thread
- ☐ Sewing machine

1 Fold the outer fabric in half lengthwise with the selvages aligned. Cut the layers 23" (58.5 cm) long for a small size, 27" (68.5 cm) long for medium to large size, or 31" (78.5 cm) long for an extra-large size.

2 Mark off 12" (30.5 cm) along the rim of a dinner plate. Place the plate over one cut end of the fabric, with one mark on the cut edge and the other on the fold. Trace the rim on the fabric, using a fabric marker. Cut on the line for a neckline opening.

3 Repeat steps 1 and 2 with the lining fabric, but cut the lining 2" (5 cm) shorter and narrower than the outer fabric.

4 Trim away the selvages. Finish the lower edges of the lining and outer fabric with a narrow double-fold hem.

5 Place the right side of the lining against the wrong side of the outer fabric. Stitch a ½" (1.3 cm) seam at the shoulder through all layers. Finish the seam allowances together by serging or zigzagging.

6 Sew the outer poncho and lining together along the neck edge with a serger, or bind the raw edges with bias binding made from the outer fabric, as for the Butterfly Blouse on page 59.

7 Pin beaded trim to the lower edges. Stitch the ribbon heading of the trim to the poncho, using a decorative stitch on your sewing machine.

Butterfly Blouse on page 59.

Now put on your poncho for instant, casual chic!

Darlene's Tips

■ Double-fold hems on slippery and slinky fabrics can be tricky, so take your time. Other options include making a rolled hem with a serger, using the rolled hem foot on your conventional machine, or if you're very ambitious, making a delicate hand-stitched rolled hem.

■ Don't throw your old soap away. Those narrow slivers make great marking tools in the sewing room.

Handkerchief Skirt

Handkerchief skirts are so feminine and romantic. Elastic waists make them super-comfortable, and they fit any figure. Handkerchief skirts can be made of anything from lightweight denims to luscious silks and velvets. Wear them for casual or dress them up for sophistication with flair.

YOU'LL NEED

- ☐ 1 yd. (0.92 m) each of two coordinating lightweight fabrics
- ☐ ½" (1.3 cm) wide elastic, amount equal to waist measurement minus 4" (10 cm)
- ☐ Tape measure or yardstick (meterstick)
- ☐ Pencil or other fabric marker
- ☐ Scissors
- ☐ Rotary cutter, cutting mat, and straightedge, optional
- ☐ Iron and ironing board
- ☐ Pins
- ☐ Thread
- ☐ Sewing machine and rolled hem foot

LET'S GET SEWING

1 Square up the cut edges of your fabric pieces so you have two rectangles the full width of the fabric and 36" (91.5 cm) long.

2 Fold the pieces in half, aligning the selvages, and layer one over the other.

3 Add 4" (10 cm) to your waist measurement and divide by 2. Stand your tape measure on edge in an arc with this measurement at the upper folded corner of the fabrics. Mark the line, and cut the fabrics.

4 Fold the underskirt right sides together, and sew the side seam from the waist opening to the selvages. Finish the seam allowances together by serging, zigzagging, or pinking. Alternatively, sew a French seam (page 58).

5 Repeat step 4 for the overskirt.

6 Time for a fitting. Pull the overskirt on up to your waist to check the size. If you can't get it over your hips, cut the opening of both the overskirt and underskirt slightly larger.

7 Put the overskirt, right side out, over the right side of the underskirt. Pin the layers together at the waist, with the seams opposite each other.

8 Serge or zigzag the waistline edges together, removing pins as you sew.

9 Overlap the ends of the elastic ½" (1.3 cm) and zigzag back and forth several times to secure the elastic into a circle.

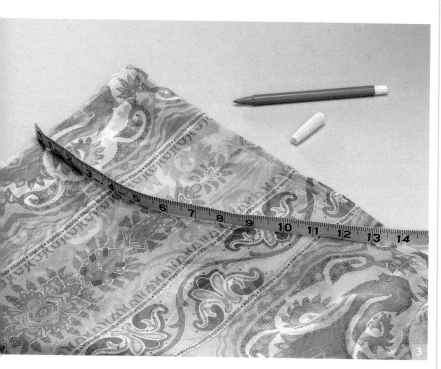

10 Pin the elastic to the inside of the waist, evenly distributing the fabric fullness.

11 Stitch the elastic to the skirt waist, using a zigzag stitch, multistitch zigzag, or serging. Stitch with the fabric on top, stretching the elastic to ease in the fabric fullness.

12 Turn under the waistline edge, encasing the elastic between the layers. Topstitch, using a stretch stitch, such as the multistitch zigzag set to its widest setting.

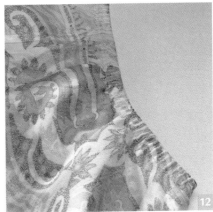

13 Using your machine's rolled hem foot, hem the lower edges of both the overskirt and the underskirt. Refer to the photo on page 59, step 10. Alternatively, turn under the edge ¼" (6 mm) and stitch close to the fold. Trim the fabric close to the stitching. Then turn under again and stitch again close to the fold to make a tiny double-fold hem.

Put your skirt on and give it a twirl!

Darlene's Tips

■ Change the look! Before sewing the waistlines together, try the skirts on and twist them around until you see the desired effect. You may want to cut the overskirt shorter than the underskirt, or cut one side shorter, for an asymmetrical look. Round the corners on one side, one layer, or all of the corners. Add a third layer. Use your imagination!

■ To help the fabric feed smoothly through the rolled hem presser foot, hold the threads with your left hand and gently pull them as you begin to sew.

Magic Yarn Scarf

You don't have to knit or crochet to enjoy the newest yarns and threads that have interesting textures and color weaves. Now, with a straight stitch sewing machine, you can enjoy these wonderful yarns as you create a fantasy fibers scarf. This stand-alone accessory will be uniquely yours and no two will ever be identical. The magic is made possible by a wonderful sewing product called water-soluble stabilizer. It will hold yarns, ribbon, and other snippets in a "scarf sandwich" while you secure them with a grid of stitches. When you dip the scarf in water, the stabilizer dissolves, leaving you with a gorgeous new fashion accessory.

Wear your creation around your neck, tied onto a handbag, or around your waist. But be prepared to make a few because once your friends see it and find out that you made it yourself, they'll want one, too!

YOU'LL NEED

- ☐ 3⅓ yd. (3.07 m) water-soluble stabilizer, 10" (25.5 cm) wide
- ☐ 5 yd. (4.6 m) each of six different yarns or ribbons
- ☐ Four pieces of parchment paper, 16⅜" × 24⅜" (42 × 62 cm) or newspaper
- ☐ Scissors
- ☐ Rotary cutter, cutting mat, and straightedge, optional
- ☐ Thread
- ☐ Iron
- ☐ Sewing machine
- ☐ Sink or bowl of water

1 Cut two pieces of stabilizer, each 5 ft. (1.58 m) long.

2 Place two sheets of parchment paper or newspaper lengthwise on a hard, flat surface overlapping them slightly. (If you use a countertop, protect it by placing a blanket or towel under the paper because you will be ironing on the surface in a later step.)

3 Place one strip of stabilizer on the parchment or newspaper.

4 Arrange narrow ribbon or thick yarn over the stabilizer near the edge to form the scarf outline.

5 Artfully arrange the remaining yarns or ribbons throughout the rectangle, some slightly overlapping the ribbon edging.

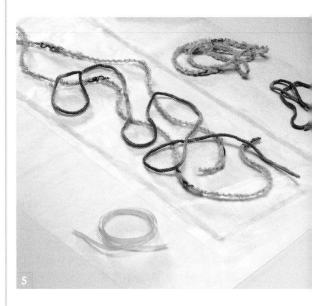

6 Cover the fiber collage with the second stabilizer strip, matching the edges.

7 Place parchment paper or newspaper over the fiber collage sandwich.

8 Press the entire sandwich, holding the iron in place for four seconds and then lifting it to move to a new position. Don't slide the iron, and be sure it doesn't come in contact with the stabilizer. Flip the sandwich and press again on the reverse side, making sure the edges of stabilizer have adhered to each other. Use a little steam, if necessary.

9 Using a new needle, stitch around the edge of the scarf, catching the ribbon or yarn outline. Then stitch lengthwise lines, about 1" (2.5 cm) apart over the entire scarf. If your machine has a quilting guide, attach it to the presser foot to help you stitch an even 1" (2.5 cm) grid.

10 Turn the scarf and stitch crosswise lines about 1" (2.5 cm) apart over the entire scarf, to complete the stitching grid.

11 Soak the scarf in water for about twenty minutes or until the stabilizer is completely dissolved. You may want to use a little dish soap to remove any residual traces of stabilizer. Gently remove the scarf from the water and rinse it in clear water. Lay the scarf flat to dry or toss it in your dryer on delicate for five to ten minutes.

Congratulations! Now you're styling!

Darlene's Tips

■ You can include snippets of fabric, silk flower petals, even feathers. Just be sure everything is caught into the scarf with a few stitches.

■ Ask your friends who knit or crochet for some of their leftover yarns.

■ Your stitching lines don't have to be straight and even. In fact, wavy lines can add a little interest to your scarf.

Swimsuit Wrap

The easiest of all apparel projects is the swimsuit coverup. Perfect for poolside or cruise ship wear, it's a versatile addition to anyone's summer wardrobe. The fabric can be a novelty net fabric, a loosely woven knit, stretch Lycra, gauze, or chiffon. Your wrap can be tied around the waist, the bust, or the shoulder with a center or side slit. It adds a touch of modesty with an element of peek-a-boo. From diving board to dining room, or from beach to bistro, you can make a graceful transition in your swimsuit coverup.

YOU'LL NEED

- ☐ 1⅔ yd. (1.58 m) fabric
- ☐ Scissors
- ☐ Rotary cutter, cutting mat, and straightedge, optional
- ☐ Thread
- ☐ Sewing machine

1 If your fabric has selvages, carefully trim them off.

2 With the wrong side of the fabric facing up, fold one long edge over ½" (1.3 cm) and crease the fold with your fingers. Then fold the edge over ½" (1.3 cm) again, and crease, forming a double-fold hem.

3 Sew along the inner fold of the hem all the way down the side, folding and finger-pressing as you go.

4 Repeat steps 2 and 3 on the opposite side and on the cut ends. That's it!

Wrap and tie for instant sophistication!

Darlene's Tips

■ If you choose stretchy fabric, stitch the hems with a twin needle, stretch stitch, or serger so the stitches won't break when the fabric stretches.

■ If you choose Lycra for your swimsuit wrap, keep a fabric softener sheet handy to wipe your work area. This eliminates static and picks up tiny lint fibers.

Tough Tote

Reusable, durable, fashionable, and customized, totes have as many uses as there are styles, colors, and sizes in which to make them. Choose a strong fabric like denim, duck cloth, canvas, or tapestry. Whether they're for groceries, beach, baby gear, overnight, books, or laundry, you can never have too many totes. These versatile bags are always a welcomed gift. Better plan on making more than one.

YOU'LL NEED

- ☐ ⅔ yd. (0.63 m) fabric
- ☐ 44" (112 cm) strapping, 1½" (3.8 cm) wide
- ☐ Tape measure or yardstick (meterstick)
- ☐ Pencil or other fabric marker
- ☐ Scissors
- ☐ Rotary cutter, cutting mat, and straightedge, optional
- ☐ Iron and ironing board
- ☐ Pins
- ☐ Thread
- ☐ Sewing machine

LET'S GET SEWING

1 Cut two 24" (61 cm) squares of fabric. Cut the strapping into two 22" (56 cm) pieces.

2 Pin the fabric squares, right sides together, along the sides and bottom. Starting at an upper edge, sew a ½" (1.3 cm) seam down one side, across the bottom, and up the other side. Pivot at the corners with the needle down in the fabric.

3 Finish the seam allowances together by zigzagging over the raw edges. Or, serge the seam allowances together.

4 Fold a bottom corner into a triangle with the side seam directly over the bottom seam. Mark a line perpendicular to the seams 2" (5 cm) from the point. Stitch on the line. Repeat on the opposite corner.

5 Cut off the triangular corners, leaving a ½" (1.3 cm) seam allowance.

6 Zigzag or serge the seam allowances together.

7 Turn under the upper edge ¼" (6 mm) and press. Then turn under again 1" (2.5 cm) and press, forming a self facing.

8 Pin the ends of one strap under the facing on one side of the tote, each 5¼" (13.2 cm) from the center. Repeat with the other strap on the other side of the tote. The straps will extend downward.

9 Stitch around the tote top along the inner fold of the facing, catching the straps in the stitching.

10 Turn the straps upward. Stitch back and forth over the straps near the top of the bag to reinforce them.

Happy toting!

Darlene's Tips

■ Before pre-shrinking your fabric, snip a small triangle from each corner. This trick will minimize fraying in the wash.

■ Want your tote wider at the bottom? In step 4, stitch the lines farther from the triangle points. Just remember this will also make the tote a little shorter.

Wine Gift Bags

A fabric gift bag is a classy way to present a bottle of wine or sparkling beverage. These bags are lined, so choose two coordinating fabrics, one for the outer bag and one for the lining. You can make three bags with as little as ⅜ yd. (0.35 m) of each fabric. Have fun with your fabric choices. Pick a design that reflects a personal interest of the receiver or sew bags from shiny or metallic fabrics for special occasions and holidays.

YOU'LL NEED

- ☐ ⅜ yd. (0.35 m) outer fabric
- ☐ ⅜ yd. (0.35 m) lining fabric
- ☐ One corded tassel set or 1 yd. (0.92 m) decorative ribbon
- ☐ Tape measure or yardstick (meterstick)
- ☐ Pencil or other fabric marker
- ☐ Scissors
- ☐ Rotary cutter, cutting mat, and straightedge, optional
- ☐ Iron and ironing board
- ☐ Pins
- ☐ Thread
- ☐ Sewing machine

Book Cover

When you give a book, you can add a custom fabric cover for a personal touch. Covers protect your books, and you can be private about what you're reading! Book covers can be made in almost any type of fabric. This cover even has a ribbon bookmark to hold the reader's place. The hardest part about making them is deciding which book to begin with, so grab a book and let's go.

YOU'LL NEED

- ☐ ½ yd. (0.5 m) outer fabric
- ☐ ½ yd. (0.5 m) lining fabric
- ☐ 12" (30.5 cm) decorative ribbon
- ☐ Tape measure or yardstick (meterstick)
- ☐ Pencil or other fabric marker
- ☐ Scissors
- ☐ Rotary cutter, cutting mat, and straightedge, optional
- ☐ Iron and ironing board
- ☐ Pins
- ☐ Thread
- ☐ Sewing machine
- ☐ Overcasting foot, optional
- ☐ Hand needle

Warming Rice Bag

When the weather outside is frightful, your rice bag will be so delightful! Just pop it in the microwave for two minutes and enjoy soothing warmth. Comfort aching muscles, a tired back, or cold feet. The removable cover has a drawstring closure and is washable. With fabrics to suit any occasion, holiday, or hobby, rice bags make a great anytime gift for yourself, your family, or friends. You'll want to try yours out tonight.

YOU'LL NEED

- ☐ ½ yd. (0.5 m) cotton fabric
- ☐ ½ yd. (0.5 m) muslin
- ☐ 24" (61 cm) narrow cording or ribbon
- ☐ 1½ lb. slow-cook raw rice
- ☐ Tape measure or yardstick (meterstick)
- ☐ Pencil or other fabric marker
- ☐ Scissors
- ☐ Rotary cutter, cutting mat, and straightedge, optional
- ☐ Iron and ironing board
- ☐ Pins
- ☐ Thread
- ☐ Sewing machine
- ☐ Seam ripper

Fringed Fleece Baby Blanket

For this charming fleece baby blanket, you'll be using not just one square, but sixty-three of them! Baby blankets are fun, fast, and very forgiving, especially when the seam allowances are fringed. The fuzzy edges get fluffier with every washing and help make this blanket a favorite cuddly comfort item. The finished blanket is 42" wide × 54" long (107 × 137 cm). Your baby blanket will surely bring smiles and be treasured for years to come.

YOU'LL NEED

- ☐ ½ yd. (0.5 m) fleece solid A
- ☐ ½ yd. (0.5 m) fleece solid B
- ☐ ½ yd. (0.5 m) fleece print C
- ☐ Paper and colored pencils
- ☐ Tape measure or yardstick (meterstick)
- ☐ Pencil or other fabric marker
- ☐ Scissors
- ☐ Rotary cutter, cutting mat, and straightedge, optional
- ☐ Pins
- ☐ Thread
- ☐ Sewing machine

1 Draw a grid on a piece of paper with seven blocks across and nine blocks down.

2 Color in the grid to represent the three different colors of your fabrics. You are designing your own quilt!

3 Place the fabric in a single layer on your cutting table. Cut twenty-one 8" (20.5 cm) squares of each fabric. Keep the squares in separate stacks.

4 Set your machine to sew a short, narrow zigzag. This will allow the seams to give a little without breaking threads when the fleece stretches.

5 Referring to your grid, place the first two squares in the top row wrong sides together. Stitch a 1" (2.5 cm) seam. Continue to add squares to complete the top row. The seam allowances will be on the right side of the blanket. Don't panic! This will become your fringe.

6 Stitch each row together, as in step 5, using your graph as a guide. Place the strips on a large table or counter in the order they will appear in the blanket.

7 Now it's time to sew all the completed strips together. Start by pinning the first two rows, wrong sides together, being careful to match the seam lines as they intersect. As you approach each intersection, stop with the needle down in the fabric to make sure the seam allowances on the top and underside are spread apart.

8 Keep adding one row at a time until the blanket is complete.

9 Go find a comfy chair. With the sharp tips of your scissors, clip into all the seam allowances up to, but not through, the stitching. Make the cuts ¼" (6 mm) apart all over the quilt creating the fringe. Also cut fringe around the outer edge.

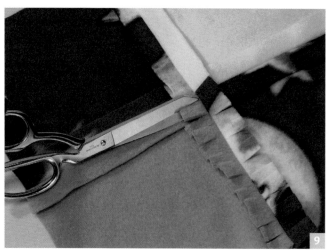

10 Wash and dry the blanket to fluff up the fringe.

Wrap it up and enjoy the smiles!

SOME BASICS

Selecting Tools and Supplies

These tools make sewing easier and more successful.

MEASURING AND MARKING TOOLS

Transparent ruler (1) lets you see what you are measuring and marking. It also is used to check fabric grain lines.

Yardstick or meterstick (2) should be made of smooth hardwood or metal.

Tape measure (3) has the flexibility to measure items with shape and dimension. Select one made of a material that will not stretch.

Seam gauge (4) is a 6" (15 cm) metal or plastic ruler with a sliding marker. It helps make quick, accurate measurements, particularly the width of

Transparent T-square (5) is used to locate grain lines and to mark square corners.

Marking chalk (6) is available as powder in a rolling wheel dispenser, as a pencil, or as a flat slice. Chalk lines are easily removable from most fabrics.

Fabric marking pens (7) are either air-erasable or water-erasable. Air-erasable marks disappear in forty-eight hours; water-erasable marks wash off with a sprinkle of water.

Narrow masking tape (8) is an alternative way to mark textured fabrics like fleece.

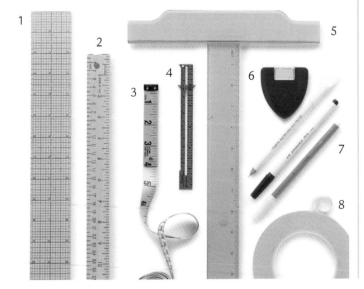

CUTTING TOOLS

It's worth it to buy good cutting tools. Use them only for your sewing, because cutting paper or other household materials will dull them quickly. Dull tools are not only a pain to work with, but can also damage fabric. Scissors have both handles the same size; shears have one handle larger than the other. Have your cutting tools sharpened by a qualified professional from time to time.

Bent-handled dressmaker's shears (1) are best for cutting fabric shapes because the angle of the lower blade lets fabric lie flat on the cutting surface. Select a blade length appropriate for the size of your hand; shorter lengths for smaller hands. Left-handed shears are also available.

Sewing scissors (2) have one pointed and one rounded tip for clipping threads and trimming and clipping seam allowances. A 6" (15 cm) blade is good for most tasks.

Seam ripper (3) quickly removes stitches and opens buttonholes. Use it carefully so you don't cut the fabric.

Rotary cutter (4) works like a pizza cutter. A locking mechanism retracts the blade for safety. Use the rotary cutter with a self-healing mat, which protects the work surface and the blade. To cut the straight lines of squares and rectangles, guide the blade along the edge of a hard, plastic ruler.

Pinking shears and pinking rotary cutters (5) are used to finish seams. They cut fabric in a zigzag or scalloped pattern instead of a straight line.

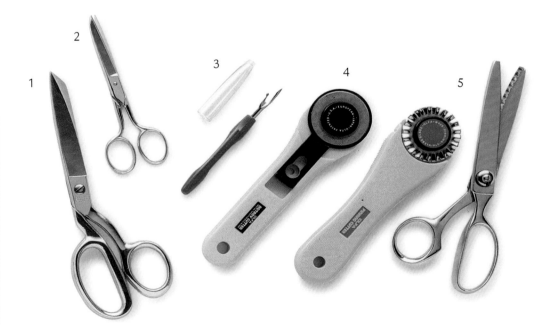

Fabrics

There are so many wonderful fabrics in the stores—which ones are right for your projects? Here are some tips to help you choose.

WOVEN FABRICS

Woven fabrics have straight lengthwise and crosswise yarns. The pattern in which the yarns are woven gives the fabric its texture and look. The outer edges of woven fabrics are called selvages. Usually they should be trimmed away; because they are woven tighter than the rest of the fabric, they may shrink when laundered or pressed. Grain lines are the directions in which the fabric yarns run. Strong, stable lengthwise yarns, running parallel to the selvages, form the lengthwise grain. The crosswise grain is perpendicular to the lengthwise grain and has a small amount of give. Any diagonal direction, called the bias, has a fair amount of stretch.

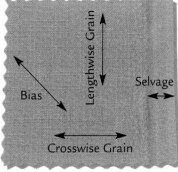

Even Weave

Twill Weave

Satin Weave

KNIT FABRICS

Knit fabrics consist of rows of interlocking loops of yarn, as in a hand-knit sweater, but usually on a finer scale. Knit fabrics are more flexible than other fabrics, and they all stretch.

CUTTING FABRICS

Cutting into a new piece of fabric may seem a little scary, considering the investment you have just made. Here are a few guidelines for accurate cutting that should boost your confidence.

Straighten the cut ends of the fabric, using one of the three methods to follow. Then mark the other cutting lines, using the straightened edge as a guide. Before cutting full-width pieces of fabric, as for the duvet cover on page 17, pin-mark the placement of each cut along the selvage. Mark out pieces for smaller projects, like decorator pillows or napkins, with chalk. Double-check your measurements and inspect the fabric for flaws. Once you have cut into the fabric, you cannot return it.

To be sure your projects will hang or lie straight, the squares and rectangles should be cut on-grain. This means that the cuts are made along the exact crosswise and lengthwise grains of the fabric. For large items, patterned

decorator fabrics are cut following the pattern repeat rather than the grainline, so the pattern can be matched at the seams.

For tightly woven fabrics without a pattern that has to be matched, mark straight cuts on the crosswise grain, using a carpenter's square. Align one edge to a selvage and mark along the perpendicular side.

For loosely woven fabrics, such as linen tablecloth fabric, pull out a yarn along the crosswise grain, from selvage to selvage. Cut along the line left by the missing yarn.

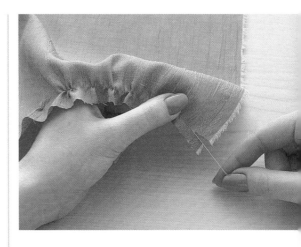

For tightly woven, patterned decorator fabric, mark both selvages at the exact same point in the pattern repeat. Using a long straightedge, draw a line connecting the two points. If you will be stitching two or more full widths of fabric together, make all the cuts at the same location in the repeat. This usually means that you cut the pieces longer than necessary, stitch them together, and then trim them to the necessary length.

Sewing Skills

Here are some sewing skills you will use over and over in the projects.

SEWING A SEAM

1 Thread your machine and insert the bobbin. Holding the needle thread with your left hand, turn the handwheel toward you until the needle has gone down and come back up to its highest point. A stitch will form, and you will feel a tug on the needle thread. Pull on the needle thread to bring the bobbin thread up through the hole in the throat plate. Pull both threads together under

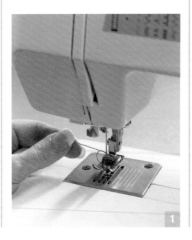

the presser foot and off to one side.

2 Cut two pieces of fabric and pin them right sides together, lining up the edges. Place the fabric under the presser foot so the pinned edges align to the ½" (1.3 cm) seam allowance guide on the throat plate and the upper edges are just behind the opening of the presser foot. Lower the presser foot, and set your

stitch length at 2.5 mm, which equals ten stitches per inch.

3 Begin by backstitching several stitches to the upper edge of the fabric. Hold the thread tails under a finger for the first few stitches. This prevents the needle thread from being pulled out of the

needle and also prevents a thread jam (a ball of tangled-up mess).

4 Stitch forward over the backstitched line, and continue sewing the ½" (1.3 cm) seam. Gently

guide the fabric while you sew by walking your fingers ahead of and slightly to the sides of the presser foot. You are only guiding; let the machine pull the fabric.

5 Stop stitching and remove pins as you come to them. When you reach the end of the fabric, stop stitching; backstitch several stitches, and stop again. Turn the handwheel toward you until the needle is in its highest position.

6 Raise the presser foot. Remove the fabric from the machine, pulling it either to the left or straight back. Cut the threads.

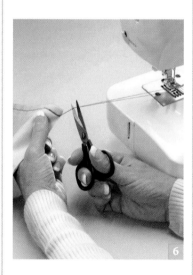

You have just sewn a perfect seam!

MORE TIPS FOR SMOOTH SEWING

■ When you insert pins perpendicular to the edge you can easily grab them with your right hand as you come to them. You are also much less likely to stick yourself with a pin as you sew.

■ Backstitching keeps the beginning and end of your stitching line from pulling out. Check your owner's manual to see how to backstitch with your machine.

■ It's easier to stitch in a straight line if you watch the edge of the fabric along the seam guide and ignore the needle.

■ You have better control of your sewing speed if you operate your foot control with your heel resting on the floor.

■ Don't ever sew over pins. You may be lucky and save a few seconds, or you could hit a pin and break the needle.

SEAM FINISHES

Everyday wear and tear on seam allowance edges will cause them to fray. To prevent this, you can finish the raw edges in one of these ways:

Stitched and pinked finish

Stitch ¼" (6 mm) from each seam allowance edge, using a straight stitch. Trim close to the stitching, using pinking shears (page 89). This finish is suitable for finely woven fabrics that do not ravel easily.

Zigzag finish

Set the zigzag stitch on or near maximum width and a length of ten stitches per inch, which equals 2.5 mm. Stitch close to the edge of each seam allowance so that the right-hand stitches go just over the edge. If the fabric puckers, try a narrower zigzag width.

SLIPSTITCHING

One hand-sewing step you will use in many of the projects in this book is slipstitching an opening closed. Here are the steps for finishing that task:

1 Insert the threaded needle between the seam allowance and the outer fabric, just behind the opening. Bring it to the outside in the seam line. If you are right-handed, work from right to left; lefties work from left to right.

2 Insert the needle into the fold just behind where the thread came up, and run it inside the fold for about ¼" (6 mm). Bring the needle out, and draw the thread snug. Take your next stitch in the opposite fold, inserting the needle directly across from the previous stitch.

3 Continue, crossing from one fold to the other, until you have sewn past the opening. Secure the thread with several tiny stitches in the seam line. Then take a long stitch, and pull it tight. Clip the thread at the surface, and let the tail disappear inside.

Sewing Terms

BASTE. Long, easy-to-remove stitches that are sewn into the fabric temporarily, either by hand or by machine.

BIAS. Any diagonal line intersecting the lengthwise and crosswise grains of fabric. While woven fabric does not stretch on the lengthwise and crosswise grains, it has considerable stretch on the bias.

BORDER PRINT. Fabric that is printed with a bold pattern, usually larger in scale than the rest of the design, running along one selvage. The border pattern is often used along the hemline in a garment, which means the lengthwise grain of the fabric runs horizontally on the garment.

CASING. A fabric tunnel that is sewn into an item to carry elastic, ribbon, or cording.

CLIP. Small, closely spaced cuts that are made into the seam allowances of a garment or other project, usually along a curve or into a corner. When the item is turned right side out, the seam allowances can spread apart and lie flat where they have been clipped.

CROSSWISE GRAIN. On woven fabric, the crosswise grain runs perpendicular to the selvages. Fabric has slight "give" in the crosswise grain.

CUT LENGTH. The total length at which fabric should be cut for a project. It includes allowances for hems, seams, and matching any prints.

CUT WIDTH. The total width at which fabric should be cut for a project. If more than one width of fabric (selvage to selvage) is needed, the cut width refers to the entire panel after seams are sewn, including allowances for any side hems or seams.

DROP LENGTH. The length of a tablecloth from the edge of the table to the edge of the cloth. It can be anywhere from 6" (15 cm) to floor-length.

FACING. A fabric extension or addition that is sewn as a backing to another piece; it protects raw edges or seam allowances from fraying and gives the item a neat, finished appearance. For instance, a jacket front and neckline have an outer layer and an underlayer, or facing.

FINISHED LENGTH. The total length of a project after it is sewn. For a tablecloth, for instance, this includes the table length and twice the drop length.

FINISHED WIDTH. The total width of a project after it is sewn. For a tablecloth, for instance, this includes the table width plus twice the drop length.

GATHER. Two rows of long machine stitches are sewn along a seam line. When the bobbin threads are pulled, the fabric slides along the stitches into tiny tucks. Gathers are used to fit a wide garment section to a narrower section while at the same time adding shaping.

HEMMING. The outer edge of a project is given a neat finished appearance by turning under and securing the raw edge in one of several methods. It may be turned under twice and stitched, encasing the raw edge, as for the edges of a napkin.

LENGTHWISE GRAIN. On woven fabric, the lengthwise grain runs parallel to the selvages. Fabrics are generally stronger and more stable along the lengthwise grain.

LINED TO THE EDGE. Backing a fabric panel with lining that is cut to the exact same size. The two pieces are joined together by a seam around the edge; the seam allowances are encased between the layers.

LINING. A fabric backing sewn to the top fabric to provide extra body and support for outer hems or seams.

MARK. Temporary guidelines or guide points that are made on the fabric for cutting, stitching, or matching seams. There are many tools and methods for doing this, such as marking pencils and pens, chalk dispensers, tape, or pins.

MITER. Folding out excess fabric at an angle to eliminate bulk. You probably miter the corners when you wrap gifts.

NAP. Some fabrics have definite "up" and "down" directions, either because of a surface pile, like corduroy or velveteen, or because of a one-way print. When laying out a pattern on napped fabric, cut all the pieces with the top edges facing the same direction.

PATTERN REPEAT. Characteristic of decorator fabrics, this is the lengthwise distance from one distinctive point in the pattern, such as the tip of a petal in a floral design, to the exact same point in the next pattern design.

PIVOT. Perfect corners are stitched by stopping with the needle down in the fabric at the exact corner before turning. To be sure the corner stitch locks, turn the handwheel until the needle goes all the way down and just begins to rise. Then raise the presser foot, turn the fabric, lower the presser foot, and continue stitching.

PRESHRINK. Fabric that shrinks, especially natural fibers, shrinks most in the first laundering. If you intend to launder your finished item occasionally, you should wash the fabric before cutting out the pieces, so the item will not shrink after you make it. "Dry clean only" fabrics can be preshrunk by steaming them with your iron.

PRESS. This step is extremely important to the success of your sewing projects. To press, select the heat setting appropriate for your fabric, and use steam. Lift and lower the iron in an overlapping pattern. Do not slide the iron down the seam, as this can cause the fabric to stretch out of shape, especially on the crosswise grain or bias.

ROTARY CUTTER AND MAT. Time-saving tools for cutting fabric; they may take a little practice and serious precautions. The blade on a rotary cutter is extremely sharp. Cut slowly, watch your fingers, and always retract or cover the blade between cuts. The rotary cutter cannot be used without the special protective mat.

SEAM. Placing two pieces of fabric right sides together and joining them along the edge with stitches. After stitching, the raw edges are hidden on the wrong side, leaving a clean, smooth line on the right side.

SEAM ALLOWANCE. Narrow excess fabric that lies between the stitching line and the raw edges. The standard seam allowance width for apparel sewing is ⅝" (1.5 cm); the standard width for home décor sewing is ½" (1.3 cm). The seam allowance gives the seam strength and ensures that the stitches cannot be pulled off the raw edges.

SEAM RIPPER. The tool doesn't really rip. Use the sharp point to slide under and cut stitches one at a time. Avoid the temptation to simply slide the cutting hook down the seam. You will inevitably cut into your fabric. Even the most experienced sewers rely on their seam rippers, because we all make mistakes sometimes.

SELVAGES. Characteristic of woven fabrics, this narrow, tightly woven outer edge should be cut away. Avoid the temptation to use it as one side of a cut piece, as it may cause the seam to pucker and may shrink excessively when laundered.

TACKING. Short stationary stitches, sewn by hand or by machine, that hold two or more pieces of fabric together and are hardly noticeable.

THREAD JAM. No matter how conscientious you are at trying to prevent them, thread jams just seem to be lurking out there waiting to mess up your day. The threads become tangled up in a wad on the underside of the fabric and the machine gets "stuck." DON'T USE FORCE! Remove the presser foot, if you can. Snip all the threads you can get at from the top of the throat plate. Open the bobbin case door or throat plate, and snip any threads you can get at. Remove the bobbin, if you can. Gently remove the fabric. Thoroughly clean out the feed dog and bobbin area before reinserting the bobbin and starting over. Then forget it and move on!

TOPSTITCHING. A decorative and functional stitching line placed ¼" to 1" (6 mm to 2.5 cm) from the finished edge of an item. The stitching is done with the right side of the item facing up. Sometimes topstitching is done with a heavier thread or two threads through the machine needle, to make it more visible; sometimes it is done with decorative machine stitches.